REAL ESTATE IN RECESSION?

The Secrets To Selling Your Home In Uncertain Times

Andos Press, San Mateo, California

REAL ESTATE IN RECESSION?

The Secrets To Selling Your Home In Uncertain Times

By Anne Dailey and Anita Schehr

FEB 1 9 1992

Published by:

ANDOS PRESS
P. O. Box 25407
San Mateo, CA 94403

3 9082 04611420 6

Copyright 1991 by Andos Press

Publisher's Cataloging in Publication Data.
Dailey, Anne J.
Schehr, Anita L.
Real Estate In Recession?: The Secrets To Selling Your Home In Uncertain Times / by Anne Dailey and Anita Schehr
Includes Index
1. House Selling   I. Title
333.33   Library of Congress Catalog Card Number: 91-71773
ISBN 0-9629374-0-1: $9.95 Softcover

CONTENTS

INTRODUCTION

CHAPTER ONE **8**

WHO ARE THE BUYERS TODAY & HOW HAVE THEY
CHANGED

First Time Buyers
Current Homeowners
Investors
Foreclosures
Out Of Town Transfers

CHAPTER TWO **16**

TARGET MARKETING

Target Marketing
Rebates
Mortgage Payment Guarantee
Home Auctions
Lease Option
Second Mortgage
Assumable Loans
FHA & VA Mortgages - Stable Mortgages
Going After Transferees
Out Of State Advertising

C O N T E N T S

CHAPTER THREE **33**

BUYER'S PSYCHOLOGY - UNDERSTANDING THE
BUYER

Psychological Reactions To Your Home
Seller's Psychological Reaction To Buyer

CHAPTER FOUR **44**

BROKER VS. FOR SALE BY OWNER

Listing With A Real Estate Broker
How To Select A Broker
Types Of Listing Contracts
For Sale By Owner
An Attorney's Role

CHAPTER FIVE **59**

SALES SKILLS FOR SELLING YOUR HOME

Strategically Preparing Your Home For The Sale
Basic Selling Skills
Negotiating Skills
Closing The Sale

C O N T E N T S

CHAPTER SIX **73**

REMODELING - PAYBACK OR PITFALL

Low Cost Improvements
Financing Your Home Improvements

CHAPTER SEVEN **84**

HIGHLIGHT THOSE SPECIAL FEATURES

Energy Conservation Tips
Buyer Handouts

CHAPTER EIGHT **89**

THE OUTSIDE & INSIDE VIEW

Guidelines To Check

CHAPTER NINE... **97**

WHAT WILL SELL YOUR HOME TODAY?

Pricing It Right
Squeaky Clean & In Good Condition
Flexibility

INTRODUCTION

To paraphrase Charles Dickens, these are the best of times, these are the worst of times. It all depends on whether you are trying to buy a home or sell a home. High unemployment and uncertain consumer confidence levels are obstacles you will need to address if you are trying to sell your home today. Now more than ever, sellers need help developing a marketing strategy that will give them a competitive edge.

Real Estate in Recession was written to be a companion guide for the home seller. It will provide you with some very innovative marketing strategies to help you sell your house, on your terms.

We'll show you the importance of pricing your home correctly and how to determine what that price should be. Learn how to use your advertising dollars where they'll count the most and how to target a specific market or buyer type.

We'll help you gain a better understanding of buyer psychology and show you how to use it to your advantage.

If you plan to sell your own home or to assist with the sale, the book will give you a crash course in basic selling skills. You'll find out how and when to negotiate, and how to close the sale.

Whether you're thinking of selling your house or you have one on the market already that just isn't moving, Real Estate in Recession will provide you with bankable solutions to help you win out.

C H A P T E R   1

WHO ARE THE BUYERS TODAY & HOW HAVE THEY CHANGED?

There are many real estate books available today that offer home sellers tips on how to market their home for a quick and profitable sale. Most of the financial and marketing plans offered are tried and true methods that work quite well in a standard real estate market. These days, however, the real estate market has changed considerably and these existing methods may not provide the results you need in today's economy.

As the market changes, sellers must adapt to those changes. To be successful you need to develop a new plan or improve on an old plan to stay ahead of the game.

What specifically has changed? For one thing the buying market pool today is smaller than in the past. Today's buyers face uncertain economic conditions and, as such, their needs and buying agenda may be different from buyers in the past. As a seller you need to adjust to this new buyer attitude.

Today unemployment figures are on the rise. It seems as though a day doesn't go by without reading about another company laying off employees and cutting back their inventory.

Recently, the Commerce Department reported that new home sales have plunged to an eight year low. Sales of existing homes dropped 5.5% in the last three months of 1990 to its lowest quarterly level in the last six years. The National Association of Realtors has recently reported a 4.5% yearly drop in sales from homes sales reported in the year 1989. This represents the lowest number of sales nationally since 1985. A low consumer confidence level and the fear of losing their jobs have slowed down the number of people looking for new homes.

Today is a very difficult time for buyers. They are trying to survive and adapt to fit the economic changes. These changes have caused consumers to make the dollars they do have stretch further. Along with that they are looking for new and innovative financial assistance when trying to purchase a home.

Economic changes will affect buyers in many different

ways. So let's take a look at the various groups of buyers and see exactly how they have changed.

FIRST TIME BUYERS

Up until quite recently coastal properties, both east and west, experienced extremely high rates of appreciation. Buyers felt confident that any house they purchased in one of these areas would provide a guaranteed return on their money. For all intents and purposes they were correct.

For a number of years houses did not stay on the market very long and sellers were getting record high profits from each sale. California buyers could be found outbidding each other to purchase a particular house, and frequently offering the seller more than the original asking price. The only category of people who suffered during the boom were first time buyers. As housing prices rose up to the sky, their hopes for ever being able to buy a home dropped to the basement.

Today, first time buyers can see a light at the end of the tunnel because of the recession. Housing prices are now lower and consequently more in line with what they can afford.

One of the issues facing first time buyers is their lack of a sufficient down payment to purchase the home they want. Further into this chapter you will find many new ideas to attract these buyers and appeal to their changing demands. The first time buyer market has enormous potential for sellers today.

CURRENT HOMEOWNERS

Current homeowners today have also needed to adjust to the economic situation. Potential buyers from this group who previously moved within their own states or counties for reasons of trading up or expanding to a larger home are now rethinking their current situations partly due to a lack of job security.

Their home value is reduced and perhaps in some instances they feel that their selling price would not offset the cost to pack up and move to a new home at this time. If they feel their financial situation is not secure they will stay put and wait to see how the economy changes.

Another segment of current homeowners who do not feel they have reason to question their job security and do maintain a financially confident outlook will see the recession as a prime opportunity to trade up. These buyers are starting to look at properties now with an eye for future appreciation when the economy improves. Their outlook is optimistic and they are prime candidates to become buyers.

The growing number of retired people are also a part of the current homeowner category. Because the purchase price of their home was so low when they originally bought it, they can be very flexible in most financial areas. For those that desire to retire out of their home state to warmer climates and to states with lower cost of living expenses, the opportunities are plentiful.

Anyone in this category who is over 55 years of age can sell their home and be able to pull out up to $125,000 which will be free from taxation. The IRS guidelines are simple to understand for this procedure. First, at least one of the owners of the home must be 55 years old on the day of the sale of the principal residence. Second, the owner must have lived in the home any three of the five years before its sale. Third, the owner cannot have used this tax benefit before. If the seller originally paid $100,000 for their home and anticipate being able to sell it today for $225,000 they would be entitled to tax free profits of $125,000 on the sale.

These people can turn out to be your buyers or they can become your competition.

INVESTORS

Property devaluation, lower interest rates and creative financing options have made this one of the best times to invest in real estate. Investors by profession who have job security, will find the time right to think about picking up prime real estate at bargain prices.

The lower home prices and interest rates will allow them to obtain a mortgage with payments low enough so that rental income will offer a positive cash flow.

OUT OF TOWN TRANSFERS

The out of town transfers category is the best buyer category today. Current economic conditions have caused a number of large corporations to cut down on the number of transferred employees, but they still maintain the policy.

A transferred employee enjoys many benefits that an ordinary buyer doesn't. If, for example, they have trouble selling their existing home, their company may buy it.

At the very least, most companies will pay the brokers fee for selling the employee's house and pick up the closing costs on the new home.

Confidence among this group is quite high because most companies won't transfer employees that they anticipate laying off. As such this category of buyer comes into your city unburdened with the problems you will find in other buyer categories.

The transferred buyer has more job security and purchasing flexibility, consequently their buyer potential is high.

FORECLOSURES

The foreclosure market is not considered a "buyer" category. It is being included here because it is partly responsible for the reduction in the size of the number of buyers today.

That reduction is a direct result of the foreclosure group increase.

The foreclosure group now includes more middle class and upper middle class people. The stability and job security normally found among these people has dropped dramatically.

These were individuals who formerly enjoyed job security and a comfortable standard of living.

In the past this group represented a large segment of the buying population. These were the people who would have traded up to larger homes.

Now, however, they are unable to move up and may possibly even lose the house they presently own. Consequently, they can end up in positions which require that they sell their home in a hurry and often times at prices lower than the market demands.

If the house should slip into foreclosure it will most likely be auctioned by a bank for an even lower price as the savings institution will only need to recoup the mortgage balance.

Having to compete against this type of bargain property is very difficult.

CHAPTER 2

TARGET MARKETING

Target marketing is the means by which you can over-come the obstacles created by today's downturned economy. Like any business or company who experiences lower sales, you need to develop a new marketing plan to fit the current conditions.

Since the first time buyer category is high on the list of potentials, we will start with this group.

Job security, and lack of a sufficient down payment weighs heavily on the minds of first time buyers. As they see the window for purchasing a home becoming larger, the rise in unemployment causes them great concern. The last thing they want is to finally purchase their dream home and then lose it because they cannot meet the mortgage payment.

Concerns of this nature are not entirely new ones for this group of buyers. Today, however, they will require a different style of marketing to capture their attention.

REBATES

The 1970's and 1980's brought about a new type of selling. This selling involved marketing plans to lure in new buyers. One of the most obvious was introduced by troubled auto manufacturers. These were called "rebates".

These marketing strategies were successful and consequently many have carried over into the 1990's. Just because you're not a manufacturer does not mean that you can't use the same tactics. Remember, first time buyers might have a problem with accumulating a full down payment and a rebate could be just the solution they are looking for.

Offering a rebate to a prospective buyer who seems interested in your home can make all the difference in the world. Certain steps should be taken in order to insure success. A rebate program for buyers can take the following form.

The buyer's offer should be made in writing to you within 12 or 24 hours of touring your home. That action would entitle them to a specified dollar amount from you, assuming you accept their offer and there is proof that they will qualify for the loan. Actual payment will be made to them at the closing of the sale when all agreements have been signed.

The rebate can constitute as little as 1/2% of 1% of your full asking price, up to 5%. If your selling price is $300,000 and your rebate is 1%, then your prospective buyer can expect to receive an amount of $3,000 from you at the closing of the sale.

Let's look at a rebate example. As a seller you have your house listed for $150,000, but you'd be happy to accept an offer in the $140,000 to $145,000 range.

A young couple is very interested in your house. They have enough money saved for a 10% down payment and associated costs, but are worried because paying out this money will completely deplete their savings. You, as a smart seller, offer them a rebate plan as follows. The couple buys your house at full asking price and you agree to rebate them $5,000. Or you will accept $145,000 with no rebate. Offer to sit down with them to explain the benefits.

Plan A: $150,000 price with a $5,000 rebate. The down payment is $15,000 balance financed is $145,000 at 9.5%

with monthly payments of approximately $1,135 for 30 years.

Plan B: $145,000 price with no rebate. Down payment is $14,500 (only $500 less than Plan A) balance financed is $130,500 at 9.5% for 30 years with monthly payments of approximately $1,097. This is roughly $38.00 per month less than Plan A.

Now the couple has a choice that will let them pay a little higher payment each month but in exchange, they now have $5,000 to put in their pocket.

Many buyers when given the choice between a $150,000 selling price with $5,000 rebate or a $145,000 price with no rebate will choose the first option.

An attorney who is proficient in real estate matters can help you put together a legal document stating the exact terms of your rebate offer.

The buyer can use the cash for many things such as increasing their down payment, paying the points on their loan, purchasing furniture, making their first mortgage payment or just increasing their savings. The point is that they can use it for anything they want. It is money that they did not have before.

"Rebate" is a term that the general public is familiar with. Your buyers might have even purchased a car from a dealership offering this incentive. Rebates are going to be attractive not only to first time buyers but to all groups of buyers. If the buyer is choosing between purchasing your home versus a house two streets over which has exactly the same features but no additional incentives, then the home with a rebate offer will be far more attractive to the buyers.

Utilizing the word "rebate" the first time you run your classified ad will attract the attention of buyers. If you are using a real estate broker be sure and ask that they use the word in their ads for your home. In print this word can make your ad stand out from the others.

As you are aware, purchasing a home takes a lot of money and your offer to give some back to the buyers can be the very incentive they need to purchase your home.

MORTGAGE PAYMENT GUARANTEE

A mortgage payment guarantee is another way to attract many types of buyers to your property.

A mortgage payment guarantee program or contract can be set up through your personal attorney. A lawyer can insure that you have the correct language in your contract and that your interests are legally protected.

The mortgage payment guarantee can take the form of offering your prospective buyers a contract that states you are willing to make the mortgage payments on their new home for up 6 months (whatever you decide you can afford) in the event that the major breadwinner is laid off from their job through no fault of their own. Most buyers will feel confident that should they lose their jobs, they will probably be able to secure new employment in this protected time frame.

The mortgage payment guarantee can run for the first year of the loan or whatever term you think is acceptable.

Like the rebate offer, the mortgage payment guarantee can be tied into a specific time frame for making the offer on your home, your acceptance of that offer and proof that the buyer qualifies for the loan.

It is a good idea to determine prior to closing the dollar amount to be allocated to this program (6 months x $1200 mortgage payment equals $7,200) and place it in some type of escrow account. Interest on the account would go to the seller.

If the buyer was laid off during the payment guarantee time period, they would receive monthly payments as outlined in the escrow instructions. The seller might want to require proof that the new home owner had applied for and was receiving unemployment payments as a method of verifying the new owner was unemployed through no fault of his/her own.

If the covered time period elapses and the program has not been utilized, the money would be returned to the seller.

Make sure you review this program with your attorney before implementing.

This contract can be signed at the bank closing of your home.

This type of incentive can take a great deal of pressure off of your prospective buyer and the odds are relatively low that your buyer will ever need to take advantage of it. However, it is something in today's economy that can provide peace of mind.

Unemployment is on the rise and the days of lifetime job security are dwindling fast. Buying a home can be a painfully hard decision for first time buyers and young couples with small children. A guarantee of this type goes a very long way towards easing the burden of purchase.

HOME AUCTIONS

The majority of home sellers will resist the idea of auctioning their houses as they consider it an act of desperation. If you are trying to sell your home and have been unsuccessful, you should look at the possibility of auctioning your home. It is only slightly more costly than a good broker. An auction can deliver a better bottom line than most people will realize.

There is an increasing number of mortgage companies who are auctioning off defaulted property and are collecting an average of 90% to 100% of the appraised value of a home. Further, you are not obligated to sell at the last bid you receive if you feel it is not high enough.

Recessionary times and slow markets can make buyers extremely cautious about paying too much for the home they buy. Consequently, the regular process of purchasing will sometimes cause them to low bid an offer or make no offer at all. An auction can push the bidding up to a higher price.

Auctions can virtually assure the homeowner of making the sale within six to eight weeks from the date you sign a contract to auction the house.

There are various methods to auctioning your home. One of the ways is to put a reserve price on your home giving you the right not to sell if the final bid offered is lower than your reserve price.

Another way to auction your home utilizes absolute bidding which means that you must accept the best offer you get. Absolute auctioning will draw a bigger crowd. You can still protect your price, however, by utilizing a minimum price at which the bidding will begin.

You can get a list of reputable auction companies from the Certified Auctioneers Institute located in Overland Park, Kansas. If you have never attended an auction of this type then you will get a better understanding of how they operate by attending one or two held from the list of those you receive. It is a good idea to check out the Sunday real estate listings for ads placed by these mortgage companies.

After you have attended the auctions and you feel that

you are interested in selling your home by this method, you should ask the company auctioning the home what commission rate is charged by them for selling homes. Check to see if they will charge you for advertising the auction of your particular home as well. Try to obtain a blank contract so that you can have your attorney go over it with you.

You can expect to pay an average of 2% of the selling price for the mortgage company's marketing efforts and another 5% to 7% as a commission. Sometimes you will have the opportunity of paying less if your home is part of a larger auction they are holding.

LEASE OPTION

A lease option arrangement is an excellent way to help buyers accumulate the funds they need for a down payment. If you have a sincere prospective buyer, but they are short on down payment funds, a lease option is something you might consider offering to help them out.

A traditional lease option is set up in the following way. The prospective buyer takes a lease on your home prior to the actual purchase. The lease period is normally one year, but can be shortened or extended if you wish.

Ideally, the monthly rental amount should cover your existing mortgage payment and taxes. To that amount an additional monthly sum is added that will be placed in a separate account to be used specifically as part of the future buyer's down payment along with any interest that is earned.

Most lease options also require that the future buyer put up a deposit, usually several thousand dollars, that stands to be forfeited if the option is not exercised. This deposit insures you have a serious prospective buyer. If the purchase does take place, the deposit is added to the down payment funds.

At the beginning of the lease period, the sales price of the house is set. You may want to be somewhat flexible in the event the current value drops or increases substantially.

A lease option tenant has far more at stake than a regular rental tenant, and as such should prove to be an ideal renter. There are however, much of the same risks that occur whenever you rent a property and you want to make sure you carefully screen any prospective tenant.

While standard lease option contracts are available

from most stationary stores, it would probably be money well spent to have an attorney work with you on putting together one suitable for your needs. That way you can be assured that all possible points of trouble are addressed ahead of time.

SECOND MORTGAGE

Another method of attracting buyers and offsetting economic concerns is to make available a second mortgage on your home and provide the home buyer with a down payment suitable to their needs.

This is not a new method of financing but an update of this strategy would include the first year of this mortgage interest free to the buyer. The remaining years of the loan can be configured to gradually increase the interest rate until the loan is repaid.

This type of loan can also be arranged with no interest due until the final year when a balloon interest payment can be made.

Any creative financing arrangements should be discussed with an attorney before implementing.

ASSUMABLE LOANS

Don't neglect to check with your current mortgage holder to see if it is possible for your prospective buyer to assume your loan. If your interest rate is fixed and is lower than current rates it will be attractive to your buyers. With the way interest rates have been running, however, odds are that your buyer can qualify for a low interest adjustable rate mortgage which can be better for their immediate needs.

FHA & VA MORTGAGES - STABLE MORTGAGES

Home sellers quite frequently depend upon FHA and VA mortgages to be the savior for their buyers.

Recent evaluations by the government of these types of loans have caused them to consider revamping the down payment policy to increase the percentage of down payment received. This is being considered in order to lessen the high number of foreclosures that the government is currently experiencing. While they might alleviate the increase in foreclosures by implementing the plan, they could also cause the shrinking buyer market to shrink even further.

FHA and VA loans are an extremely crucial means of financing homes for middle and low income groups. The lower down payment required for this type of financing has saved the day for many, many buyers.

A new type of mortgage recently being discussed on the West Coast might well be what your buyer should consider. This new mortgage is called the Stable Mortgage. It is a hybrid that combines adjustable and fixed rates into the same mortgage contract. There are two options currently being discussed.

One option would carry three-fourths of the loan amount at a fixed rate, with the rest of the loan carrying an annually adjusted rate with a 4% lifetime cap. Another option would carry half of the loan at an adjustable rate and the rest offered at a fixed rate. The adjustable lifetime cap for this version would be 6%. These mortgages will require a minimum of 10% down.

It is anticipated that this type of mortgage will be available in late 1991. Contact major lenders in your geographic area to see if they are offering this type of financing. If they do, make a note of the lender. Your prospective buyers may not be familiar with it and you can help to point them in the right direction.

GOING AFTER TRANSFEREES

If you have signed up with a nationally affiliated real estate agency you will automatically be able to target this group of people. However, you need not depend solely on the connections of your real estate firm.

Your local library can provide you with a listing of the top 100 companies on a national level. Write a short cover letter to the Human Resource Departments of each of these firms stating that you are putting your home up for sale. Include a best feature listing of your home and neighborhood school locations as well. Enclose a picture of the front of your house. If you are offering financial assistance, a rebate or a guarantee this should be listed first.

Ask these companies to keep the information regarding the sale of your home on file and give it to any transfered employee moving into your area within the next 6 months. Most personnel departments will be glad to comply with your request.

OUT OF STATE ADVERTISING

Out of state advertising in major metropolitan newspaper is also a way to get the attention of potential transferees. Select the states where large corporations are headquartered. Most newspapers have a classification entitled "Out Of State Properties" which is where you will want your ad to run.

To insure that your ad will be noticed you will want to get ad rates from these newspapers for Classified Display Ads. Classified display ads will be larger than the usual liner ads listed. In addition you can request a border to surround your ad to call more attention to it.

Headline your ad with the most important feature in a larger type size then the remainder of the ad. If you are offering a rebate or some other incentive you should use this as the headline of the ad. The adtaker you speak to will help you select the standard type sizes used by the newspaper. Ask that a copy of the printed ad be sent to you upon publication.

If you want to receive calls only at certain times of the day, remember to take into account time zone differences.

Some major metro newspapers publish their own Sunday supplement magazine for insertion into the delivery. They might also run a back page of this publication listing homes for sale along with a photo. If your home is priced in a higher bracket, this vehicle can be used to advertise your home out of state very effectively.

The strategies listed in this chapter will help to distinguish you from other home sellers. A home seller today needs to be innovative in their selling techniques as well as practical. A buyer's market demands that you, as a seller, be informed and knowledgeable as well as flexible with your terms.

CHAPTER 3

BUYER'S PSYCHOLOGY - UNDERSTANDING THE BUYER

Buying a home is for the most part a very emotional decision. Each buyer has his or her own set of psychological "hot buttons" that will affect their decision making process. As a seller it helps to be aware of these feelings so you don't create any unnecessary obstacles or add to any already present anxiety.

There are many different types of buyers. They include first time buyers, young families, families moving up the economic ladder, single buyers, empty nesters (couples whose children are grown and out on their own) and retired people. Each type has its own unique needs and problems, although some needs are common to all types.

First time buyers have many compelling reasons for wanting to purchase a home. These include the desire to stop paying rent and to start building equity, to have a place of their own which they can customize and decorate as they desire, and to put down roots and establish some permanence in their lives.

For first time buyers the financial commitment of buying a home can be a very scary thing. The down payment required to purchase a home today usually amounts to a very sizeable sum of money. Obtaining the down payment comes after considerable scrimping and saving, borrowing from family, or perhaps a combination of both. Once the money is accumulated, parting with it even to purchase a home, is an anxiety ridden process. These buyers want to be assured they are making a sound decision.

What can you do as a seller to help alleviate some of the stress? If the sales transaction is being handled by a real estate agent, they should be prepared to deal with these items. If you are selling your house yourself then you need to be aware of possible buyer concerns and visualize how you will handle them. The first guideline is to remain calm and project a relaxed manner at all times. You never want to come on too strong or apply too much pressure.

Keep in mind that before the first time buyer began to look, they most likely wrestled with the financial issues.

They may only need to be reminded of their own conclusions. Ask what made them decide to buy a house now. Focus back on their comments agreeing with the good points they make. By using the buyer's own rationale you can overcome any cold feet you might encounter.

For the move-up or repeat type buyer, jitters are not as much of a problem. This is a more confident buyer who is familiar with the process. For this type of buyer, the emotional factors will dwell less on the financial aspects and more on moving and leaving behind the house that has become home. Very often children will be involved and there is the emotional turmoil of leaving friends and possibly changing schools. You can help this type of buyer by being knowledgeable about your community; investigate school locations, both public and private, as well as academic standings. It's always helpful to know how many children are in the neighborhood and their ages. A child concerned about moving always loves to hear that there is a little boy or girl their age who lives nearby.

Adults can also find moving stressful. This is especially true for corporate transfer moves. By learning a prospective buyer's interests, you can let them know what your community has to offer. Do they like to play golf? Let them know if there are good courses nearby. Are there social clubs, city sponsored recreation programs? Maybe your community has outstanding medical facilities or adult education programs. By asking a few simple questions you may uncover some "hot buttons".

For empty nesters or retirement buyers convenience and security will be important. If you live in a safe, low crime area be sure to let them know. Is there a neighborhood watch program? How about special senior recreation programs? Emphasize the proximity to stores and services, if it exists. Also don't overlook good public transportation as a selling feature.

All buyers, regardless of type, will want the reassurance that they are making a sound financial investment. A well maintained home, in a safe, friendly neighborhood will go a long way towards convincing them that they are making the right decision. A smart seller will do everything possible to project their house in this manner.

PSYCHOLOGICAL REACTIONS TO YOUR HOME

As a buyer tours your house they will receive tremendous sensory data that will ultimately create a negative or positive reaction. Obviously you will want

36

your home to be spotlessly clean and free of clutter. A neat and clean interior provide an overall well-maintained image that is very beneficial. There may be, however, some less obvious things that will create a very strong emotional response.

First on this list is color. Color has an overwhelmingly strong impact on your emotions. Think of the last time you bought a car, remember how important color was in your decision making process. You can find the exact model you want, with all the required features, but if you don't like the exterior color you're not going to buy the car.

When selling a house, color can be equally important. Strong colors will elicit strong reactions. Some people will love a bright purple bedroom, but others will hate it. As a seller you can't risk alienating anyone, so the best advice on color is to keep it neutral. While off-white walls may seem terribly boring, they rarely ever offend anyone. A buyer can more easily visualize the colors they like when viewing a neutral-colored room, than when viewing one that is strongly colored or wallpapered.

This is especially true when it comes to visualizing their furniture in your home. A neutral carpet and wall color will allow almost any furniture color, but it is hard to imagine a soft peach sofa in bright red room. Remember that despite individual color preferences, certain colors create the same physiological responses in everyone. Many shades of blue and green are relaxing. You don't have to personally like the color to experience the sensation. Hospitals frequently use these colors to provide a peaceful, calming atmosphere. Red, on the other hand, is very stimulating. It's a favorite color for sports cars. Yellow generates a warm, cheerful feeling because of its association with sunlight. Lighter colors will create the feeling of openness and space while dark colors have the opposite effect. Use color effectively and it will help you sell your house. Color is so important because it is perceived through one of your most vital senses: sight.

When considering the emotional impact your house will have on prospective buyers, go through each of your five senses and see how your house interacts with each one.

Another sense that creates a strong impression is smell. Here again it is best to remain as neutral as possible. Even pleasant smells can cause negative reactions. Think of what it is like to be in an elevator with someone who over did it on perfume or after-shave. Even though the odor of the fragrance may be pleasant, there can definitely be too much of a good thing. This is frequently the problem with room deodorizers.

Unpleasant odors should be avoided at all costs. These would include heavy cooking odors, odors from smoking, pets, medicinal or antiseptic smells including ammonia-based cleaning products. These types of smells will cause a negative emotional response.

The most positive smells are those associated with freshness and cleanliness. Open your windows and let in as much sun and fresh air as possible. Besides being the best overall room deodorizer, it's free. Letting the sun in will actually eliminate mildew and musty smells. Fresh cut flowers help bring the best of the outdoors inside. When cleaning or dusting use a lemon based cleaner or furniture polish. Lemon has a light odor that is much more acceptable then ammonia.

Continuing with our sensory inventory, let's consider hearing. If you want a buyer to concentrate on your home's finer points, you want to eliminate any distracting noise. When touring a home, silence can be golden. Peace and quiet can provide a feeling of calm and security. Most people want their home to be a haven from the hustle and bustle of the world, try to create that atmosphere for your prospective buyers.

When buyers are present, don't run the dishwasher or any other noisy appliance. Keep the TV off. Music, if carefully chosen, can be very helpful. Most people associate music with happy, pleasant times and it can make us relax. However, the wrong music or any music played too loudly will be a turn-off. If you decide on background music, keep it neutral and soft.

Before you show your house test your doors and windows for undesirable squeaks; oil any noisy offenders. Don't let squeaks and/or drippy faucets undermine your home's well-maintained image.

Touch and taste will play lesser roles in the sensory relay, but don't overlook them. As a buyer tours the house, they will touch or handle a great many items. Everything should be clean, dust or grease should never be encountered. You'll also want to enhance the well maintained image you've created - make sure everything is sturdy and solid to the touch. Eliminate any loose towel bars, cabinet doors and light switches.

Taste, as a true sense, will play the smallest role, but still give it some consideration. An offering of food or drink can create a warm, friendly impression. Have some ice water, tea or coffee available as well as some guest-type cookies, crackers or candy.

We all form our opinions based on the sensory data we receive, so cater to all five senses when readying you and your home for a buyer's visit.

Another vitally important emotion to consider is that of trust. Psychologically a seller must create an atmosphere of trust. Any attempt to deliberately conceal flaws will backfire. If you have things that require repair, bring them up yourself - don't let the buyer discover or uncover them. Once a buyer feels deceived, you can never re-create a feeling of trust. Not only should the buyer feel they can trust you, but you need to indicate that you trust them as well.

When buyers tour your home, don't follow right on their heels, watching their every move. Give them a little room, never invade their personal space. To give you the peace of mind you may need for this, make sure that any small valuables or extremely personal items have been removed to a safe place. Touring someone's home can be a very awkward situation and you want to do everything possible to make the buyers feel comfortable.

SELLERS PSYCHOLOGICAL REACTION TO BUYER

Now that we have looked at the buyer's reaction to your

home, let's look at the seller's reaction to the buyer. Perhaps the single biggest mistake a seller can make is to make wrongful assumptions about a buyer. Remember the old adage: don't judge a book by its cover. Nothing could be truer when it comes to judging buyers.

Never rule out a buyer because they don't dress the way you do. It's impossible to judge a person's financial means by the way they dress or the car they drive. To let a prospective buyer know that you don't take them seriously or that you question their financial means can cost you a sale.

Even obvious lookers should be treated courteously and with respect. While they might not be potential buyers themselves, they might know of someone who is. If they are treated rudely, you can be sure they won't relay any favorable information about your home. So it is critical that you treat each and every person who tours your home as a true possible buyer.

Along the same line, never assume that a single person may not be a serious prospect. Single people are one of the fastest growing consumer groups today. They do buy houses! Another dangerous assumption is that the husband will make the decision. Most couples buying homes today have and require two incomes. Decision making will most likely be a shared responsibility.

Avoid gender classifications when showing your home. Don't assume that only a woman would be interested in the kitchen or that a home office will be more intriguing to a man.

In summary, try to keep in mind the five senses as a mental preparation for yourself. Making a wrongful assumption can quite possibly cost you a sale and last but not least, the best advice is to treat everyone who looks at your house in a courteous manner and view them all with an open mind.

C H A P T E R 4

BROKER VS. FOR SALE BY OWNER

There has been a long standing debate about individuals selling their own houses versus listing their home with a real estate broker. There are those who will argue that complex issues combined with time consuming efforts will not result in much money being saved by trying to do it all themselves.

The purpose of this chapter is not to provide you with a definitive answer, but rather to provide you with information to help you make the right decision for yourself.

In the past, market conditions have been more favorable for people selling their homes without the aid of a real estate agency. Today's economic conditions can make trying to sell your home without professional help more difficult but certainly not impossible.

LISTING WITH A REAL ESTATE BROKER

The business of listing and selling your home with a professional and reputable real estate broker can ease the burden of a cumbersome process. These professionals are educated and trained to provide a high level of service. Once you agree to list your home with a real estate agency, they will be working solely for your benefit.

Some of the broker's duties will include advertising and promoting the sale of your home. They will photograph and document the features of your house and provide this information to prospective home buyers as well as other real estate agencies who are members of a multiple listing service.

Since their business is selling homes they will be able to make use of long standing contacts both locally and nationally as part of their efforts to provide the best service. Their years of experience can pay off in tangible benefits to you by offering the best advice on the methods of preparing your home for showings, as well as pricing it right for the sale.

A professional agency will handle any objections that are presented by prospective buyers and utilize sales strategies that have proven effective in the past. Your broker is prepared to deal in a professional manner with all types of personalities.

A broker will qualify buyers for you so that your time, as well as their time is not wasted on prospective buyers who cannot afford your home.

They will assist the buyer in making an offer on your home while protecting the interests of the seller. A real estate agency will assist in filling out loan applications as well as provide information regarding the bank or savings institution which will best handle the buyers' needs.

A real estate professional will automatically follow up on every stage of the process so that you, the seller, can use your time preparing for the physical move itself.

If you are an individual whose lifestyle requires frequent travel, listing with a real estate agency will allow you to maintain your daily schedule with minimal interruption. The assistance they will provide to you is invaluable under these conditions.

All of these reasons and more will justify the cost for listing with a real estate broker. But all real estate brokers are not created equal. Since the broker will be handling your most valued possession it's a good idea to interview several firms before you select the one right for your needs.

HOW TO SELECT A BROKER

In today's market it is more important than ever before to find the right agency for your home sale. You will be looking for the firm who is the most creative and imaginative in their marketing techniques, a firm whose financial contacts reach well beyond the local bank around the corner, as well as a proven record of success for home sales in your area.

If there is a particular real estate agency whose signs consistently say "sold" in your neighborhood, then you should make this your first stop. Look in your local newspaper to see which brokers advertise the most and which ones consistently use larger, more elaborate ads.

Compile a list of best possible brokers and contact each for an appointment. As you interview each broker ask who their most successful agent is and how much the total dollar value of the property they sold in the previous year was. Ask who has been most successful selling homes in your particular area. Ask what percentage of

47

those homes that were both listed and sold by the agent. Ask if that agent would be available to represent you in the event you select their firm to list your home.

Find out what percentage of commission they charge for selling a home and ask if all advertising costs are included in the commission fee.

Find out about the relationships they have with banks and savings institutions and their success ratio for securing loans. It might be a good idea to ask if they will consider using part of their commission as a loan to a buyer who might need help with the down payment.

While you are there it is a good idea to check the multiple listings for the price range of homes recently sold in your neighborhood. Once you have that information ask the broker what the average listing price of homes are that this particular real estate firm specializes in. It's best to sign up with an agency who deals frequently in the sale of homes in your price range.

See if you can obtain the names and phone numbers of a few people who have recently listed and sold their homes through this particular agency. Contacting these people to check their satisfaction level is a good method of acquiring confidence in the broker you finally select.

These steps can be taken repeatedly through several brokers compiled on your list. Select one or two of these and make an appointment to have an agent come to your home to present you with a proposal to list and sell your home.

Ask this broker to include the suggested asking price justification, the commission to be charged, as well as the type and term of the listing. The agency should also provide you with their proposed marketing techniques and an honest opinion of your home's sale potential. Lastly, ask the broker why he/she believes that they can sell your home.

As a homeowner you should be cautious and careful about creating an unintended legal obligation between you and the broker. Oral or inferred remarks may be enforceable under some state laws even though they are not in writing.

TYPES OF LISTING CONTRACTS

There are several different "types" of listings that a broker might offer.

An Open Listing means the seller has the right to retain

as many brokers to represent him as he/she wishes. The seller retains the right to sell the property without obligation for commission to the broker, unless that broker was specifically involved in securing the buyer.

An Exclusive Listing means that only one broker will act on behalf of the seller. The seller will retain the right to sell the property without obligation to the exclusive broker unless the broker was already involved with securing the buyer.

An Exclusive Right To Sell means only one broker is selected as the sole agent of the seller. This broker has absolute and exclusive right to sell the home. The seller will be obligated to pay a commission to the broker even if the seller brings in his/her own buyer and is responsible for the sale.

A Multiple Listing contract is the same as the exclusive right to sell. The only exception is that the exclusive broker is given the additional right to distribute the listing to all brokers who are members of a multiple listing organization. The seller is obligated to pay the broker an agreed upon commission. The broker will share that commission with the member of the multiple listing organization who is responsible for the sale.

As you can see, the choices appear to be many. However, you will probably discover that your selected broker only handles listings through an exclusive right to sell or through a multiple listing contract. You may think that having an open listing would be the better approach using the theory that the more people who see your home the greater the odds are that you will be able to sell it. In reality the use of multiple brokers in listing your home is not very practical. Even if you could find some who were willing to list your home this way, odds are that they would feel the competition between brokers would be too great and consequently not worth the effort of actively showing your home.

A successful broker who uses only multiple listings can create the same effect as an open listing with greater protection for the broker's firm. By giving the information on your home to other members of the multiple listing organization you increase the odds of finding a buyer for your home.

FOR SALE BY OWNER

People have been selling their own homes without professional assistance for generations. Today's downturned economy means that you will need to work harder to be successful at it.

The most obvious reason for not using a real estate agency would be the potential savings from not paying a commission. When buyers were in abundance and the economy was in better shape this fact was a good reason for selling your own home.

You might find that today, however, most buyers will expect a "for sale by owner" home to have a lower asking price than an equivalent one listed with a real estate agency. Consequently, pricing your home correctly will be the most important thing you need to undertake. Nobody wants to pay too much.

A very inexpensive way to check the current asking and selling prices of the houses in your neighborhood would be to visit a local real estate office. Ask if you might be able to look at their multiple listing guide. Telling them that you are simply interested in the average selling prices of homes in your neighborhood for the purpose of securing a home equity loan should open up the door for you. Looking through a broker's multiple listing books can give you most of the information you need. However, some real estate offices do not let the general public have access to this information.

Another way to check current market values is to hire a professional appraiser. The cost for this service will depend upon the size of your home. You can expect to be charged somewhere between $200.00 and $400.00 for this service. You might wish to contact the mortgage loan officer at your bank for a list of suggested professional appraisers you can contact.

If either of these two methods do not appeal to you then you should probably consider driving to the courthouse in your county where you can look up the information you need free of charge. Go prepared with the addresses of some recently sold homes in your neighborhood.

Selling your home yourself will mean that you will be handling and arranging everything. Consequently, you might find the intrusion into your personal and business schedule difficult to accommodate.

Composing a classified ad, as well as paying for it, will be your responsibility when you are selling your home yourself. In addition to correctly composing your ad you'll need to determine exactly where the prospective buyer will phone for information on your home. Placing your personal home phone number versus your business phone number will need to be decided by you.

If phoning your home directly is the only choice then you might consider purchasing an answering machine (if you don't already have one) so that the prospective buyer can leave their name and phone number for a call back. Some states are now offering a system of phone answering directly through your local telephone company. This method is inexpensive. It does not require the purchase of a physical piece of hardware and can be discontinued immediately when it is no longer required. There will be a nominal installation and monthly service charge for this system.

Another responsibility you will undertake in selling your home yourself is to screen and qualify the prospects that have called in response to your classified ad. A simple way to accomplish this is to ask a few direct but simple questions.

Using a conversational tone ask where the buyer is from and how soon they need to purchase a home. Inquire into their method of financing the house. Will they be using a government sponsored loan such as a VA, FHA or are they seeking a conventional method of financing? Try to ascertain if they already own a home.

You'll also have to screen your prospects to be sure that your personal safety as well as the possessions in your house will be maintained. There are no guaranteed methods of accommodating this need over the phone. The best suggestion would be to arrange your showings when other members of the household are home. If you live alone consider having a friend or neighbor with you during showings.

If you are selling your home yourself it is a good idea to prepare by phoning banks and savings institutions to inquire about current financing available. Ask for loan application guidelines as well as current rates. You might just need to coordinate the loan process for your buyer if they are unprepared to do it themselves.

Another step you might want to take care of ahead of time is to get a Structural Pest Control Report (termite inspection) as most buyers today will be required to have one by their lending institution.

AN ATTORNEY'S ROLE

Finding as attorney who specializes in real estate will be an important matter to attend to. Once you have decided on a particular lawyer, ask what opinions and descriptions they have of the sales process. It is good idea to get a blow-by-blow account so that you have a complete understanding of the process.

Advise the attorney you select that you desire him or

her to not only read the sales contract or offer, but to represent you in any contract negotiations with your buyer's attorney. You will also want representation at the bank closing of the sale.

If you are planning to arrange any financial assistance for the buyer yourself, you will need an attorney to assist you as well. He or she will also be needed when you are required to arrange for a title search. Will this attorney contact a title company and make all the arrangements?

Ask your attorney what happens if you receive any earnest money. Does this mean that you are legally bound to accept their offer? Will you have to take your home off of the market? Ask your lawyer for his or her recommendations.

Find out if your attorney will provide you with the necessary documentation you will need such as sales contracts or a pre-printed offer form.

Some nationally affiliated real estate agencies offer a Buyer's Guarantee. You might feel that putting together your own version will give you an advantage. This type of guarantee allows buyers to feel confident that if any concealed or previously unknown damage should come to light after they purchase the home then you guarantee that the necessary repairs will occur at no expense to the buyers. There will be a lot of research to undertake regarding the physical stability of your home if you decide to offer such a guarantee. Is your attorney familiar with such a process and can he or she provide you with guidelines as well as a physical contract of guarantee?

Last but not least, inquire into the fee that will be charged.

ALTERNATIVE METHODS

If you are undecided about the necessary commitment required to sell your home yourself, you might want to take advantage of outside services that are prepared to assist you. A company like Help-U-Sell will charge a flat fee and will assist you with necessary forms, writing your ad, and providing you with a For Sale sign as well as other services.

They do provide advertising through mailings which will list your home along with others in your immediate area and are sent out when requested by buyers who phone for the information.

This cost will be somewhat less than signing up with a

real estate agency and could provide you with an additional level of assistance as opposed to going it alone.

Information about Help-U-Sell can be obtained by calling 1-800-660-4357.

Once you establish a firm commitment to take on the responsibilities of selling your home yourself you can be successful. The control over the sale will be in your hands and the attorney you select can help you over the rough spots.

C H A P T E R 5

SALES SKILLS FOR SELLING YOUR HOME

A recessionary market will require a lot of imagination, preparation and skill to sell your home. If you have decided to try your own hand at this game there is one other thing that will come in very handy. It's that good old standby, common sense. Let's start with the strategic preparations you'll need to make.

STRATEGICALLY PREPARING YOUR HOME FOR THE SALE

Strategic plans can be pretty basic. One of the best ways to make your house stand out among a crowded field is to make all needed repairs before the for sale sign goes up and not during the selling process. If you can accomplish this step you will be well on your way.

If for some reason you just cannot or do not have the time to make a specific repair or perhaps several major repairs then you should be the first to point this out to your prospective buyers. If your buyer has to point out needed repairs to you during the tour of your home, you will not be getting off on the right foot.

Beating your buyers to the punch can be accomplished by giving your prospective clients a handout that lists the repairs you fully intend to make in the event they decide to purchase your home. Sign and date the list before you hand it to your prospective buyers. It will become an official document that your buyer will respect.

In addition you will accomplish several other things by the use of this handout.

First, it will let them relax about your intentions to make repairs. Second, it will allow them to feel that you have shared a truthful confidence with them. Third, they will begin to trust you. After all, they don't know you and you have just taken a step in the right direction.

This one action alone can make your home stand out among the many houses they have looked at.

Of course, selling a home that is neat and clean is mandatory, but you should be prepared to go beyond that point. Don't neglect to store away any material that might be construed as offensive such as adult publications. Many prospective buyers can be easily turned off to your home for just such a reason. They may not bother to tell you why they are not making an offer as they leave your home.

Your home should be inviting and pleasant. But above all it should be a neutral zone so store away any contraversial political or religious items. When you home is for sale it should not be an advertisement for personal beliefs or political causes.

Once you feel confident that you have all your bases covered regarding the preparation of your home, you can move smoothly into the selling process.

BASIC SELLING SKILLS

If you don't have any formal training in sales you should not let that deter you. You can be taught basic selling skills given enough time. What you might not have now though is enough time to hone the art. This chapter will give you the "quick and dirty" points of the time honored tradition of selling.

You might be familiar with the old saying that you can't teach an old dog new tricks. That saying is dead wrong. You just need to remember to keep it simple and you can accomplish anything.

The simplest and most basic skill to learn about selling is to listen. The process is simple, ask a question and then listen to the answer. As basic as this concept is some people can never get the hang of it. They will conjure up a mental picture that a salesperson's job is to sell and, therefore, a good salesperson should constantly be talking about whatever it is they are trying to sell. It all boils down to knowing when to talk and when to listen. There you go, you are now privy to the best advice about being successful in sales.

Now that you have the secret to selling you need to sharpen your skills. The best way to do that is to understand how to ask a probing question. There are a lot of different types of questions. There is a direct question such as "are you going to buy my house"? There is an accusing question such as "will this check bounce"? And then there is a probing question like "do you and your wife enjoy making a cozy fire during the winter"?

This type of probing question will do a lot of things for you. First of all it will give you the opportunity to confirm that your prospects have noticed a particular feature about your home. Second, you will give your buyers an opportunity to relax a little and open up to you. Third, it will bring about an interaction with your buyers that will let you mention other features they might have missed. Fourth, you will be subconsciously planting the wonderful little seeds of "purchasing" in the minds of your buyers without sounding like a broken record.

A probing question will also help you deal with a silent buyer. A little silence is good, sometimes it can mean that your buyer just needs a little bit of time to form an opinion about you. If you think that you are nervous about selling your home, remember that the average buyer is usually far more nervous.

Every once in a while you will run into buyers who might be just plain shy. Other buyers might think that by keeping silent they are secretly pounding away at your psyche. They'll be successful if you let them. Try helping them open up a little bit by using the probing question method and then listening very carefully to the answer.

On the other hand there will be times when you'll wish you did have the silent type, especially when you encounter buyers who are overly inquisitive. This is especially true when the conversation concerns anything personal in nature, or if the questions are focusing on a topic you'd like to stay quiet about.

Nobody likes a bragger. While this is a blunt statement it's especially true when you are trying to sell your home to strangers. Don't overstate your personal feelings about your home.

Nobody wants to listen to a constant stream of how much you and your spouse will miss the house and you really wish you didn't have to move. You'll be putting your buyer in a position that may be uncomfortable for them and force them to silently disagree with you. Buyers need to feel that it is their own decision whether or not your home is right for them.

This doesn't mean, however, that you can't sell the benefits of your home. Mentioning that you recently had all the floors and woodwork in the home revarnished is not bragging. It is, however, letting the buyer know that they will not have to attend to that type of maintenance for quite some time.

Any personal reasons you have for selling your home that involve a divorce, an illness in the family or a recent death will either depress your buyers to the point that they can't wait to leave your property, or will give them a signal that you are desperate and are probably willing to give them the deal of the century.

Remember the earlier advice of keeping things simple, now is the time to apply it. Keep your answers brief and simple. If a buyer wants to know what your reasons are for selling your home, don't go into a long detailed explanation. A nice, appropriate response is merely to say that you want to move across town to be close to your office, closer to the airport, or perhaps closer to your aging parents.

Being transferred to another state can also give your buyers the wrong signal. If it is at all possible keep your furniture in place as long as you can. An empty house does not sell as well as a furnished one. And once again that huge, green, flashing light will blind your buyers.

If it is just not possible to leave your furniture in place, you might want to consider contacting a furniture rental company as your interim plan. These companies can provide a single room of furniture for a relatively low monthly cost or they can provide furniture for your whole home. The latter will be quite expensive. If it helps to sell your home it will be worth the additional expense.

NEGOTIATING SKILLS

Along with understanding basic selling skills you'll need to learn when and how to negotiate the sale of your home.

Even novices to the art of negotiating can take a liking to it. There is nothing finer than thinking you are making out like a bandit. In order to get that kind of high out of a very stimulating activity like negotiating, you'll need to act like you've been doing it for years. This means, of course, that you won't make the mistake of offering giveaways at the first sign of a negative impression from your buyers.

Giveaways are not a form of negotiating. Giveaways are simply things you give up with nothing in return. Negotiating is a give and take process. If you give something away then you should expect to get something in return. Don't risk prematurely losing your negotiating power, save it for when you need it, which will be at the close of the tour of your home.

There will be plenty of time as your buyers go through your home to make a mental list of items you will be able to negotiate on if they are serious about purchasing your home. Pull out those basic sales skills you just learned and listen to the remarks being made by your prospects. What may appear to be an obstacle for them at first can be turned into a positive remark if the discussion is handled properly by you.

Turning a negative remark into a positive remark can be accomplished by using a probing question. As an example, let's imagine that your buyers are in your living room. They have just encountered their first "problem" and it appears to be the color of your draperies. Listen first to what comments are being made and then step into the conversation by asking "what color of draperies would go best with their furniture"? By asking this question first you will accomplish several things.

First, you will start a discussion of the color of drapes they would prefer to have. This will usually lead into a discussion about how their couch and furnishings go so well with the particular color of draperies they would like to have.

Second, your participation in the discussion will lead them to believe that you have an interest in how they live and what would please them.

Third, you will have turned their negative impression on the wrong drapery color into a pleasant, positive discussion about what color they would really like to have.

Fourth, you will have demonstrated your willingness to make a deal without seeming to be anxious and most importantly, without actually making the offer to replace the drapes. Be sure to make a mental note of this conversation because if they are interested in your home your willingness to purchase their selected drapery color will become part of the negotiated deal.

Fifth, your probing question will have set the stage for proper negotiations when the time comes. Remain relaxed and positive at all times and remember to smile.

CLOSING THE SALE

There is another old saying that goes something like this. Never assume, if you do you will end up making an ass out of you and an ass out of me. While that may be a bit graphic for some people's taste, it nevertheless is sound advice.

Never assume that it is a done deal because your prospects seem to be agreeing with everything you say. It could be that they just don't want to be rude and really don't like your house at all. You can avoid this by looking for the right signals and confirmation from your buyer that they would like to proceed. How do you do that? Use the probing question method and listen very carefully to your buyer's response.

Your questions should be subtle, direct and probing all rolled into one. A good example of this is to ask at the end of the tour if your buyer feels your house is a place their family could be happy in. If their answer is yes then obviously you will need to take the next step.

The next step is to close the sale. During the closing process you will want your buyers to feel confident about your home. What will help to put them at ease is your friendly and relaxed manner.

Suggest that they sit down at your dining room or kitchen table to go over any questions they might have. If they agree to this step the closing process has already started.

If they are not serious they will simply thank you and leave or worse yet they will leave you with the fatal words "we will get back to you later in the week". At this point you should definitely not stop showing the house.

When the question and answer session seems to be at an end and your buyers have not verbally offered to purchase your home, you will need to take the bull by the horns. If you have explained in detail your rebate, mortgage payment guarantee, assumable mortgage, etc., end the presentation with the fact that you can only validate your specific offer by receiving their offer to purchase within 12 or 24 hours. Ask if you can expect to receive an offer from them in that time frame. Follow the specifics listed in Chapter 2 Target Marketing.

If the buyer elects not to take advantage of a rebate program but would rather negotiate the price, then join in the negotiating process. Try to end negotiations by requesting an intent to purchase check along with their official offer to purchase your home.

Both seller and buyer should remember that the check is a sign of good faith and will remain uncashed. When the loan process is completed, or if the buyer elects not to purchase the home the check will be returned to the buyer.

It should be understood by your prospects that during the loan application process you will continue to show your home to others. The reason for this is that it may take a couple of weeks for your buyers to get verification from a lending institution that they qualify for a loan. During this time, if you continue to show the house, you might receive another offer you can use as backup should the first offer fall through.

If there is a contract or official agreement relative to your guarantee or rebate then have it prepared and ready for them to sign. Give your buyers a copy of the agreement as well as a copy of their offer.

As mentioned in an earlier chapter, have an attorney draw up the contract or agreement so that you as well as your buyers are legally protected.

INSPECTIONS

State laws will vary regarding the required inspections of your home. A pest control report along with a structural engineering evaluation might be required or requested.

You might want to have the results of any specialty inspections such as a structural engineering report, asbestos, radon, etc., ready to give to your buyers.

The National Association of Realtors is currently lobbying for legislation which would require home sellers to provide full disclosure to their buyers on the condition of their property.

In the final analysis understanding basic selling skills, being prepared to negotiate at the proper time, handling the closing of the sale and making sure that your attorney has reviewed any special circumstances is essentially all there is to it.

By paying attention to your buyers and listening carefully to what they say, you will be successful in your efforts.

C H A P T E R 6

REMODELING - PAYBACK OR PITFALL

Many homeowners today who are considering selling their home think that it is necessary to engage in expensive remodeling projects in order to get a higher price for their home.

Property conditions today play a far greater role in a home sale than it did two years ago when it was a seller's market. The condition of your property determines not only whether or not buyers will buy, but it also determines the price they will pay. Always remember to attend to needed repairs first before you plunge into major remodeling projects.

If you choose to remodel during the current recessionary period, you may find yourself suffering if prospective buyers make an offer for your home that does not meet your incurred expenses or your expectations.

It is always a good rule of thumb not to exceed 20% of

the current value of your home. In today's market that can sometimes be difficult to stay ahead of. What may be a fair market price when you initially lay out your plans for remodeling, could end up being overpriced by the time the project is complete. Naturally, the bigger the project the longer it will take to complete it.

Remodeling projects that take longer than 45 to 60 days to complete will raise your risk and decrease the odds of getting a good return on your investment. This might happen if housing prices continue to drop while the construction is being completed. A recession in real estate is definitely not the time to engage in a major overhaul of your home.

A typical 45 to 60 day remodeling project might include adding another bathroom to the existing floor plan. Perhaps dividing a larger bedroom into two smaller ones. Enlarging the small alcove in your bedroom into a private dressing area or perhaps even a computer corner/small office.

Like most investments, there are good ones and bad ones. The greatest return on your investment will be in updating or upgrading your kitchen. Buyer interest in modern kitchens is high. If your kitchen is more than 20 years out of date then your investment in remodeling it should provide excellent returns.

Total kitchen remodeling can include new mid-range priced cabinets or a refacing of existing cabinets, laminate or tile counter tops, and an energy efficient oven with cook top and ventilation system. You should either replace your dishwasher with one that has energy and water saving features or add one if there was none. Replace the kitchen floor with a good tile covering. Replacing the garbage disposal and adding recessed kitchen lighting will increase the value of your home as well. The remodeling costs recouped should be 100% or more.

A kitchen remodeling project, if properly planned by an experienced contractor, should not take more than eight weeks from start to finish.

If your kitchen has been remodeled within the last ten years then simply updating some of your kitchen appliances will improve the salability of your home. Adding items such as a garbage compactor, a ceiling fan or under cabinet lighting will greatly appeal to the average home buyer. It's a good idea, however, not to go overboard in this regard because major improvements on top of already improved areas won't return your total investment dollars.

Remodeling bathrooms should also return your full investment. If you undertake this project you should install new lighting, replace your older medicine cabinet with the new, larger mirror designed cabinets, and replace or professionally refinish your bathtub. Other items you should replace are your sink, vanity stand, and the commode. You might want to add ceramic tile to replace the older bathroom floor.

Adding a second bath is also a good investment. Sometimes this can increase your payback by twice your original investment. This is especially true if you have increased your bedroom count from two to three or three to four.

Adding additional closet space, closet organizers or a storage area will always appeal to your buyers. In addition it will usually pay back 100% of your investment. Buyers love plentiful storage space.

Another short term improvement you might want to consider is adding an entry hall if one is not present in your home. The majority of buyers today want an entry hall in the home they buy. Consider the possibility of creating the illusion of one. If the entrance to your home goes directly into your living room you can accomplish this illusion by removing a 4 foot by 4 foot area of the wall-to-wall carpeting immediately in front of the door. Replace this carpeting with a good ceramic or marble tile and you will have created a small entry point for your family as well as your guests.

Another means of creating the illusion of an entry hall would be to add a 3 to 4 foot high divider next to the inside of the front door. If you use molding in a geometric pattern on the divider you can highlight and customize it. Repaint it to match the color of your walls.

Creating a pass-through between the kitchen and dining room is another short term remodeling project. By doing this you will make this area appear more spacious.

If your home has a basement you might want to consider turning that area into a comfortable play area for children as well as adults. This project will be less costly than adding a whole new room. Your investment dollars will be protected and the additional space will be attractive to your buyers.

If you decide to improve your basement area, then stick to the basics and you will keep your costs down. Simple things like using a suspended ceiling to cover heating ducts and pipes instead of calling in the carpenters and replastering will keep your costs down.

Insulate the walls in your basement and cover them with

an attractive panelling or perhaps use wallpaper over prefabricated drywall. These tips will help to keep your costs low.

Lay down a good tile floor and use inexpensive area rugs to provide a more cozy feeling. This will give the area a clean and finished look as well. You will be providing easy maintenance for your prospective buyers who have children and pets.

If the laundry area is located in your basement don't consider moving it to another room in your home unless the additional higher costs are part of your budget. The cost to lay in new electrical and plumbing lines as well as new fixtures can be quite high.

You can separate the laundry area from the remodeled room by either constructing a new wall or blocking off the view by using a room divider.

Improving the visual appeal of the outside of your home might mean you are considering a landscaping project. These types of projects can give you a high rate of return providing you don't overspend. If you add a red-wood deck with an average cost of $5,000, you can expect a return of 80% to 100% of that amount.

If your home is more than 40 years old, then you might

want to consider replacing older windows and doors with energy efficient ones. Replacing these items can be quite costly but it certainly adds salability and appeal to the buying market. You might also want to consider adding an exhaust fan and extra insulation to the attic which can give you a good dollar return. In addition, these things can lower your heating and cooling costs which should be of great interest to today's buyers

LOW COST IMPROVEMENTS

Almost every real estate book you read today will advise you to make sure all your curtains are open and the lights are on when you are ready to show your home. This is good advice, but what if your house doesn't have a lot of windows? Adding track lighting to the ceilings in the living room can have the effect of adding depth and dimension as well as lighting to the room. This is a simple, low cost project that you can probably accomplish yourself.

Low cost improvements such as adding smoke alarms, new light fixtures, replacing light switches with dimmers, and replacing older locks with new deadbolt locks will add salability and safety features to your home.

Replacing bathroom or kitchen wallpaper in a more up-dated pattern or perhaps repainting the walls will appeal to your buyers and keep your investment low.

Adding a bright outside light and a low level lighting system around walkways and paths can help to add a three dimension look to your yard when landscaping is not plentiful. Use solar lighting if possible since there will be no electrical usage required.

Don't forget to include your bathroom in low cost improvements. Replace towel bars with brass or porcelain towel racks. If possible add a brass built-in magazine rack. Add shutters to the bathroom window.

Do-it-yourself improvements under $100.00 can include things such as putting chair-rail or cornice molding around your dining room or living room. Paint this addition to either match existing walls or wallpaper shades. Replace doorknobs with brass, porcelain or cut glass. You will be amazed how small things can brighten the look of your home and make things look new.

If your bedroom doors are flat and not distinguishable then add moulding in a 4 or 6 panel design. Repaint the doors afterwards. The effect will be striking. Replace older plastic electrical switch and outlet covers with brass or porcelain. These projects will add improvement but will not usually total more than $100.00.

FINANCING YOUR HOME IMPROVEMENTS

There are many fixed-term installment loans which can be a quick route if your remodeling plans require more cash than you currently have access to.

Fixed-term installment loans are usually under $25,000. This type of loan can last from five to ten years and they might require a less rigorous credit process check as well. Depending upon your current financial situation this could be the preferred manner of financing.

A home equity loan or line of credit can be used for more expensive projects. Home equity loans will usually have a longer pay back period and will use open ended terms. You will probably pay about the same interest rate as the fixed-term installment loan, usually 1 to 2 points above the prime rate for both types of loans.

Don't neglect a government sponsored low interest loan for any energy related and home improvement projects which are available to middle income homeowners. For information you can write for the Consumers Guide to Home Repair Grants and Subsidized Loans from the

Consumer Education Research Center, 350 Scotland Rd., Orange, NJ 07050 or call 1-800-872-0121. The cost of the book is $10.95 plus $2.00 for shipping. The total cost of your capital improvements (permanent improvements that add value to your home i.e., new roof, kitchen remodeling, etc. can be added to the original (tax basis) price of your home. When you sell the property, you will reduce the taxable gain by that amount.

The Internal Revenue Service will require proof of the expenses that were incurred for any capital improvement projects and used to increase the tax basis of your home when you sell it. It is advisable to keep every receipt. The IRS does not allow you any consideration for your own personal labor costs when you do it yourself.

The buying and selling of real estate has significant income tax consequences. Many times the income tax aspects are more important than the price of the property. Income tax aspects of a real estate transaction should be considered before the sale, not after. Once a sale takes place, it is too late to go back and restructure the sale to take advantage of any tax laws that were overlooked.

Income tax laws are complicated and constantly changing. Before entering into a complicated real estate

82

transaction, you should seek the advice of an income tax specialist, such as an attorney or accountant.

Whether you are going to repair, remodel or replace, with today's downturned economy it is best not to over spend and to use common sense. Is there anything that your home does not have that you wish it did have? Even small, low cost improvements will increase the attractiveness of your home.

Buyers today want value for their dollar just like they did in the past. The only difference is that today's dollar is worth considerably less. Stretch your dollars when you consider remodeling and you won't get caught in the pinch.

C H A P T E R   7

HIGHLIGHT THOSE SPECIAL FEATURES

Many homes have special features that deserve recognition. Highlighting these features will be important to your prospective buyers. Special features usually fall into categories such as energy conservation, environmental protection, and health and safety. As a home seller you should highlight any features that relate to these items.

To determine what features you can highlight, survey your house paying particular attention to your appliances, heating and cooling systems, home insulation, etc. As you conduct your survey, write down any energy saving features you discover.

If your home is energy efficient then by all means state that it is. Is the attic insulated with a minimum of R-30 insulation materials? If so, put this on your list along with the dollar amounts of your heating and cooling bills. Today's energy conscious buyers will consider this an important factor.

Are the outside walls of the house insulated? Are there storm windows? Have you recently recaulked the windows? Have you taken measures to assure that no air sneaks inside the house because of ill fitting doors? Have you installed a ventilator fan in the attic to move out hot air in the summer? Have you fixed leaky ducts and pipes? Is your home equipped with a heat pump? All of these things are important sales features for buyers today.

Are any of your appliances energy efficient? If so then be sure to include them on the list. Most appliances purchased within the last five years have special settings for energy conservative customers. If yours comply then be sure to highlight them.

If your washer and dryer are up for sale or are part of the purchase of your home, then be sure any energy conservation features they have are listed. This is also a good time to note if warranties are still applicable on any of the appliances you've listed. Be sure to indicate any purchased service contracts, as well as the name and phone number of the local repair company.

If you have installed a water filtration system be sure you list the manufacturer when you note it on your list.

A water filtration system can save the prospective buyer hundreds of dollars every year by eliminating the purchase of bottled water.

If you live in the part of the country where earthquakes occur, then list the measures you have taken to protect your home from damage. Have you had the house bolted to the foundation? Can you provide them with an engineering report stating that your house is up to code for the particular state you live in? If you have covered any of these items, be sure to include them on your list.

Have you recently had your home waterproofed? This will be especially important if your home is built of stucco or wood.

Outside solar lighting is also very important to today's buyers. People like the security of outside lighting, but don't necessarily like the idea of higher electric bills to support the feature.

On the environmental side, asbestos and radon are issues of great conern.

If your home is free from asbestos in the insulation, ceiling, floor covering or pipes, let your buyers know. You can contract for this type of inspection and have the report available for your prospective buyers.

Buyers are also concerned about unsafe levels of radon. Radon is a radioactive gas that you cannot see or smell. Constant exposure to unsafe levels of radon can present serious health risks. It is considered to be the leading cause of lung cancer deaths in non-smokers.

Radon seeps into houses from soil and rocks through cracks in the walls and foundations. The Environmental Protection Agency (EPA) has surveyed 34 states, so far, and has found the highest percentage of unsafe levels in the following states: Maine, Massachusetts, Pennsylvania, Ohio, Indiana, Wisconsin, Iowa, Minnesota, North Dakota, Nebraska, Kansas, Wyoming, Colorado and New Mexico.

Fortunately, you can easily and inexpensively test for radon yourself. You'll need to purchase a charcoal-based radon detection canister or alpha track detector which should be available at a local hardware or drugstore. Be sure to purchase one that has passed the EPA proficiency test. Testing directions will be included in the kit.

If the test evaluation shows levels of radon that are of concern, the EPA office or local American Lung Association can suggest radon-reduction measures.

By now you should have a pretty good idea of what features can be called out. Prepare a neatly typed list covering your homes special highlights. Have enough copies available so you can hand one to each prospective buyer as they walk through the door.

It could be a mistake to assume that your buyers will be able to identify all of your home's features. To emphasize them, point out each item on the list as you come to it on the tour of your home. If your buyers see as well as read these things you will have a better chance that your home will be remembered over others they have toured.

C H A P T E R   8

THE OUTSIDE AND INSIDE VIEW

It has always been true that a neat and clean house will sell quicker than one that gives the appearance of being unkept or soiled. Today's recessionary market means that your home must be exceptionally clean.

If your home is priced right to sell, you can raise the odds for a quicker sale by having the outside as well as the inside of your home in tip top shape without any exceptions.

The first impression you make on prospective buyers will be the "look" the outside of your home presents to them. The following outside guidelines will help you make a favorable impression.

OUTSIDE GUIDELINES

* If house numbers are not clearly marked purchase brass numbers to be placed in an easily viewed area on the front of your home.

* Use a spray fertilizer on your lawn & water well.

* Cut lawn so that it is no shorter than two inches. Be prepared to do this every 4 days.

* Trim bushes and hedges to a respectable height. Make sure that the front door can be seen clearly from the driveway or street.

* Invest in some low cost pottery that can be filled with bright flowers. Put these flower containers on the approach to your door or on the porch.

* Your garage door should be closed before their arrival.

* Make sure all your automobiles are either in the garage or parked down the street away from your home.

* If you have an electric garage door be sure it is working properly.

* If the view of your home is blocked by a neighbor's vehicle or boat consider an arrangement whereby the vehicle or boat is moved to another location.

* Put children's toys and bicycles away.

* If the driveway has unslightly oil stains consider investing in a gallon of light grey concrete paint. If your driveway is blacktopped then have a fresh sealer coat applied.

* Obvious cracks in the driveway or walkways can be of unwarranted concern to buyers. Repair them as soon as possible.

* If a wooden fence or gate is visible from the street restain or repaint it, if necessary.

* Wash all outside windows and screens in the front and back of your home.

* Make sure that all gutters and drain runoffs are free of debris.

* If your house is built of stucco or brick there might be stress cracks that are obvious. These should be repaired immediately. Small stress cracks are fairly common, but

can cause concern for prospective buyers.

* Paint or restain the front door to your home.

* The screen door should be free of dents and scratches.

* Open and close your screen and front door. If squeaking noises are present spray the door with oil.

* Make sure the door bell works.

* If there is a porch light fixture clean it well and check to be sure the lightbulb works.

* If there is a lightpost in your yard consider cutting out a foot of the lawn surrounding it and filling in with redwood chips, white stones and/or bright flowers.

* Touch up the paint if shutters appear worn and repair any damaged areas.

* If roof shingles are missing or damaged purchase replacements.

* Be sure your yard is free of any pet droppings.

* Flower or vegetable gardens should be free of weeds.

* If the rear yard has been used as your storage area for leftover things, clean it up and remove anything offensive to the eyes.

* If any trees are growing into electrical or telephone lines either call the city to trim them back or arrange for an outside service.

* If you have motion detector lighting be sure they are working properly.

INSIDE GUIDELINES

The inside of your home shares equal importance. It needs to be spotless. Consider hiring a professional cleaning service for a really thorough once over. Weekly upkeep visits might also be worth the expense.

Avoid clutter at all costs. Rent storage space if you need to.

During showings it is best if children and pets are out of the house. Try to refrain from smoking to avoid unpleasant odors as well as any possible allergic reactions in your buyers.

93

The following inside guidelines can be used as a checklist.

* Make sure your rooms are light and bright. If not, open the drapes and pull up the blinds.

* If you don't have lots of windows make sure the room or rooms are painted a pleasant white or off-white. The lighter walls will give the appearance of being brighter and more cheerful.

* If there is a guest closet in your entry hall or living room make sure it is clean and neatly organized.

* Buy some brightly colored flowers and put them on display in a pretty vase.

* Is the room overly decorated with too many pictures or wall hangings? Take some of them down and store them away.

* If items are removed from the walls be sure and patch up any nail holes or marks and repaint over the area.

* If you have a fireplace be sure to clean out any burned wood and ashes. Fireplaces can be the focal point of the room.

* If your dining room area is small and your dining room set is too big for the room, move it out of the house temporarily. It is better to have less furniture in a room then to have it appear overstuffed and too small.

* Your kitchen should be absolutely spotless. Make sure your burners on top of the stove are clean and free of food spills.

* Make sure your refrigerator is free from old/moldy foods and vegetables.

* Wash and wax the kitchen floor.

* Make sure your garbage container in the kitchen has been emptied.

* Rooms that have low light or little sun can be brightened by increasing the wattage in the lamps or ceiling light.

* If you smoke be sure that all ashtrays are clean.

* Don't leave dirty laundry or bath towels in clear view. The bathroom should be as spotless as your kitchen.

* Don't leave stockings hanging on the shower rod.

* Bathroom cabinets should be clean and uncluttered.

* Bathroom towels should be clean and neatly hanging on the towel rack. Purchase a new set of towels that you bring out just for the prospective buyers.

* Check shower doors and door glides for unslightly buildup.

* If the toilet has stains purchase a bottle of bleach and let it stand in the bowl over night.

* Make sure the bathroom windows and window sills are clean.

* If you use your bathroom for your kitty litter box change the location.

* Bedroom closets and storage areas should be clean and not overstuffed.

CHAPTER 9

WHAT WILL SELL YOUR HOME TODAY?

There are homes for sale all around the country today that have been on the market for more than several months. There are also some homes for sale that are experiencing relatively quick turnarounds. Why are some homes selling faster than others in a recession? The answer is really very simple. Homes that are selling are priced right, they are clean and in good condition and the sellers are flexible about their terms.

PRICING IT RIGHT

Pricing your home right means not exceeding what the market will bear. Today's market description translates into the following formula. Whenever there is a housing downturn that approaches deep recession levels (the last one occurring in 1982) and there is a drop in the new construction of single family homes, the market becomes buyer oriented and prices of existing homes for sale will drop. In some areas of the country home prices have not hit bottom yet. Other areas have shown slight increases in home sale activity.

This all means that if you are serious about selling your home today, your home cannot be overpriced. By pricing your home accordingly, you will broaden the range of buyers who are going to be able to afford to buy your home. All types of buyers today will recognize the window of opportunity a recession offers to them.

Homes that are selling today are selling within 95% of their listing price. This occurs because they are priced right. There are several ways to find out exactly what your home is worth today. Some of these are listed in Chapter 4. Other ways include carefully monitoring market activity. This is accomplished by asking your real estate agent to collect Realtor Estimates of Value. A REV is simply another agent's opinion of the salable price of a home. Realtor Estimates of Value can occur if your listing agent is a multiple listing member. As other broker/agent members tour your home when it first comes on the market, they will be able to provide their opinions regarding the price of your home. If this immediate feedback indicates that you are only likely to receive 80% of your asking price you can then make the adjustment immediately or apply the difference in the form of a rebate or guarantee as listed in Chapter 2.

Being able to accept up front that your home has gone down in value is paramount to being successful. It doesn't matter that Jack and Sally's home just down the street sold for 25% more last year than you can ask for your home today. Times have changed and you will need to get past the idea that you are losing money on the sale of your home. Any sale that will allow you to recoup your down payment and pay off the mortgage is not losing money. If you plan on purchasing a replacement home, you should remember that you will be paying less for that home as well.

If your profit margin is slight or non-existent and the sale of your home absolutely must occur, then you should revert to something like a lease with an option to buy or even a straight rental lease. As undesirable as these options might be for you, it will be better than losing everything. Remember, the market will not stay down forever and as the economy gains strength you can place your home up for sale at that time.

If you are not in a hurry to sell your home and you can't bear the thought of not having a high margin of profit then do not put it on the market now. You will end up wasting the time of a lot of people including yourself.

SQUEAKY CLEAN & IN GOOD CONDITION

While pricing your home right is one of the most important steps to take, don't forget that the condition your home is in will affect the price as well.

Chapter 6 details the value of remodeling versus the cost and also provides low cost tips for improving the condition of your home. Chapter 8 details absolute necessities to be attended to both outside and inside your home. Having two chapters devoted to this subject was intentional. You cannot afford to try to sell a home in bad shape today. Not unless, of course, you are literaly giving it away.

Now is the time to view your home from the perspective of the buyer. Keep in mind that the buyer is currently king and has a vast selection of homes from which to choose. Stressing any outstanding features your home has by the use of handouts as discussed in Chapter 7 can make your home more appealing to the buying market.

FLEXIBILITY

A home seller today needs to remain flexible with their selling terms. Flexibility can take many forms as was discussed in Chapter 2 Target Marketing. Understanding that successful home sales today will fall within the boundary of receiving 95% of the asking price means that the balance of 5% is open for you to try to negotiate in some form. Recognizing this inevitability will allow you to become imaginative in your terms.

If your buyers were attracted to your home because your classified ad indicated a rebate or guarantee of some sort then you might be able to recoup 3% or more of a lower than expected offer. An appealing incentive of cash directly back to the buyer might convince them that offering your full asking price is acceptable. If your buyers qualify for the purchase of your home at 95% of your asking price, then chances are that they will qualify for the loan at 100% with 1 or 2% of that coming back to them in cash.

The amount or percentage of the sale price that you return back to the buyer, via a rebate, will of course depend upon how much your home is worth. Houses selling for $400,000 with a 1% return to the buyer will mean $4,000 they can use to purchase furnishings, use as part of their down payment, or perhaps use this money to pay the loan points.

Less expensive homes can accomplish the same amount back to the buyer by increasing the percentage accordingly. First time buyers and others who are short on cash will think twice about whether they desire a mortgage $4,000 or $5,000 less which will result in a very minor lowering of their monthly mortgage payment or having cash in their hands when they need it.

Naturally, you can forego this form of incentive and simply agree to the lower offer made on your home if that will serve your interests in a better way.

Today's recession demands that your home be priced right. Buyers will be scrutinizing your home at a much greater level so it should be in the best possible condition. That and flexibility in negotiating terms with your buyer will make your home sale successful and quick.

INDEX

Advertising: 31-32, 53-55
Appraisal: 52-53
Asbestos: 86
Assumable mortgage: 28
Attorney: 21-22, 27, 55-57, 83
Auction: 23-25
Basic sales skills: 61
Basement: 77
Bathroom: 76
Broker: 45-49
  alternative to: 57-58
Buyer psychology: 33
Closing the sale: 68-71
Color: 37-38
Current homeowner: 11-12
Earthquake: 86
Energy conservation: 84-85
Entry hall: 76
Environment: 84
Exclusive Listing: 50
Exl. Right to Sell: 50
FHA: 28-29
First time buyer: 10
Foreclosure: 14-15
For sale by owner: 44, 51-52
Handouts: 60, 84, 88
Home Equity Loan: 82
Inside guidelines: 94-96

Inspections: 71-72
IRS: 12, 82
Investors: 13
Kitchen: 75
Laundry area: 78
Lease option: 25-27
Listing contracts: 49-51
Low cost improv.: 79-81
Mtg. payment guarantee: 20-22
Multiple Listing: 50-51
Negotiating: 66-68
Open Listing: 50
Outside guidelines: 89-93
Pricing: 52-53, 97
Probing question: 63-64
Psychology
  buyer: 33-36
  seller: 41-43
Radon: 87
Rebate: 17-20
Retired: 12
Remodel: 73-83
Sales skills: 59-65
Second. Mtg.: 27
Senses: 36-41
Stable Mortgage: 29
Target marketing: 16-23
Transferee: 13-14, 30
VA: 28

O R D E R   F O R M

R E A L   E S T A T E   I N   R E C E S S I O N ?
The Secrets To Selling Your Home In Uncertain Times

Please send _____ book(s) of Real Estate In
Recession at $9.95 each to:

NAME _____

ADDRESS _____

CITY _____

STATE _____ ZIP _____

*CA residents add 7% sales tax.

**Shipping & Handling Book Rate $1.75 1st book
plus .50 each additional book. Air Mail $2.50
per book.

Send Check or Money Order Only To:

ANDOS PRESS
P. O. Box 25407
SAN MATEO, CA 94402

Book Total	$ _____
Shipping	$ _____
Sales Tax	$ _____

Sales Tax applies to CA residents only

TOTAL ORDER $ _____

Allow 4 to 5 weeks delivery time